Horrible Jobs in

ANCIENT GREECE and ROME

Gareth Stevens
Publishing

ROBYN HARDYMAN

Please visit our website, www.garethstevens.com.
For a free color catalog of all our high-quality books,
call toll free 1-800-542-2595 or fax 1-877-542-2596.

Library of Congress Cataloging-in-Publication Data

Hardyman, Robyn.
Horrible jobs in ancient Greece and Rome / by Robyn Hardyman.
  p. cm. — (History's most horrible jobs)
Includes index.
ISBN 978-1-4824-0329-9 (pbk.)
ISBN 978-1-4824-3306-7 (6-pack)
ISBN 978-1-4824-0328-2 (library binding)
1. Occupations — Greece — History — Juvenile literature. 2. Occupations — Rome
— Juvenile literature. 3. Greece — Civilization — To 146 B.C. — Juvenile literature. 4.
Rome — Civilization — Juvenile literature. I. Haryman, Robyn. II. Title.
HD4902.5 H37 2014
937—dc23

First Edition

Published in 2014 by
Gareth Stevens Publishing
111 East 14th Street, Suite 349
New York, NY 10003

© 2014 Gareth Stevens Publishing

Produced by Calcium, www.calciumcreative.co.uk
Designed by Simon Borrough
Edited by Sarah Eason and Rachel Blount

Cover Illustration by Jim Mitchell

Photo credits: Dreamstime: Andyemptage 24r, Costas1962 15, Creapictures 8, Fazon1
44, Garydyson 9b, Gretasplace 22, Lagui 40t, Mytime 16, Nmaverick 17, Paul837
23, Paulcowan 9t, Tinka 37, Trilobite 7; Getty Images: Superstock 38; Shutterstock:
AdrianNunez 43, Bertl123 34, John Copland 5, Kamira 6, Lagui 26, Morphart Creation
32, Hein Nouwens 10, 28, Lefteris Papaulakis 19, PavleMarjanovic 45, Bill Perry
25, Tatiana Popova 21, Andrey Starostin 33b, Darren Turner 40b, Cedric Weber 4;
University of South Florida: 18; Wikimedia: Caliga10's 41t, Peter Clarke 36, Ecelan 31,
MatthiasKabel 12, 27, Marie-Lan Nguyen 13, 14, Prioryman 39b, Pascal Radigue 30,
Shakko 33t, Johnny Shumate 20, Giorgio Sommer, Naples National Archaeological
Museum 39t, Steff 11, Vassil 42, Walters Art Museum 24l, WolfgangRieger 29.

Printed in the United States of America.

CPSIA compliance information: Batch #CW14GS: For further information contact Gareth Stevens, New York, New York at 1-800-542-2595.

Contents

Chapter One
Ancient Greece

The civilizations of ancient Greece and Rome have had a huge influence on the Western world. For more than 1,000 years, from about 500 BC to AD 500, first the Greeks and then the Romans flourished in lands around the Mediterranean Sea and far beyond.

The National Gallery, in London, England, is an example of how the Greek building style has been copied all over the world.

Magnificent and Ordinary

As early settlements grew into towns and cities, the jobs people did became more varied. Not everyone had to work simply for food and shelter. More specialized work was carried out by craftspeople, traders, and builders. Some people became richer. This was how great civilizations started.

By the time of the ancient Greek civilization, people were creating magnificent buildings and inventing literature and other forms of culture. Greek ideas of philosophy and politics are still used today. Yet, still these things were done by a small group of people.

Simple Lives

Most people lived simpler lives in ancient Greece. For them, life was hard work. And for some people, the jobs they had to do were really horrible!

This painting is at the palace of King Minos, at Knossos in Crete.

Really Ancient Greece

Greek civilization began as far back as 2000 BC, on the island of Crete in the Aegean Sea. There the Minoan people traded with neighboring lands and farmed the rich soil. Their biggest city was Knossos, which had paved roads and an enormous palace for the king, Minos.

Work in Greece

Greek civilization was at its peak in the fifth century BC. At this time, Greece was made up of many separate areas, called city-states. The biggest and richest city-state was Athens. Sparta and Olympia were others. The city-states sometimes fought each other but joined together to fight against their common enemies.

Working in Athens

Athens was very wealthy. Its wealth came from trade, from taxes paid by other countries, and from mining. The main port, Piraeus, was buzzing with business. While some people got rich, most people just earned a living by doing an ordinary job. For example, every town had a pottery area in which potters made and decorated pots for everyday or special use. In fact, much of what we know about life in ancient Greece comes from the paintings on the many pots that have survived.

This beautiful vase is painted with a scene of a chariot and rider.

Wages for Work

Coins were introduced into Greece in about 600 BC. They had been invented in Lydia, in modern Turkey. Each city-state made its own coins. They were usually silver and stamped with the symbols of Greek gods. Some jobs were paid with coins, but lowly jobs were sometimes paid in goods, such as food.

This silver Athenian coin shows an owl, a symbol of the goddess Athena.

Having a Say

The ancient Greeks invented the idea of democracy. This is when the people get to have a say in how their country is run. However, in ancient Greece this right was not available to everyone. Only citizens could take part in the decisions, and not everyone was a citizen. Women weren't allowed to vote, and neither were foreigners or slaves.

Poor Peasant

A lucky few ancient Greeks were wealthy. They lived mostly in the towns, and had plenty of slaves to serve them. Most people, however, lived as poor peasants, trying to make a tough living on the land. For them, life was a constant struggle to survive.

Lousy Land

Greek soils were not fertile. The land was rocky and the small villages were often separated by mountains. Peasants struggled to grow just enough to feed their families. The main cereal crop was barley. A community often had to share just one ox to plow their land, and families took turns using the animal to pull a simple wooden plow for sowing crops. Farming tools were very basic, and using them took endless hours of muscle power. Crops often failed in the poor soil—and if a farmer got into too much debt, he could even be sold into slavery!

Life as a poor peasant in ancient Greece was hard.

The poor peasants also kept a few animals, such as sheep and goats. These provided wool, milk, and some meat. They also kept bees, for honey. The land was mostly too rocky to keep cattle. Fortunately, the sea was never very far away, so peasants could catch fish.

Greek land was more suited to keeping animals than to growing cereal crops.

Olive Oil

One plant that grew well was the olive tree. Olives were harvested in late fall, then pressed to make olive oil. This was used for cooking, and in lamps for lighting. However, it takes 20 years for a newly planted tree to produce olives and that's a long wait when you have a hungry family to feed.

The area around Athens was famous for its groves of olive trees.

Sold into Slavery

In ancient Greece, as in all ancient societies, slavery was seen as normal. Slave traders brought people from outside Greece, for example from Asia Minor and North Africa. They were shipped to Greece and sold as slaves at the market. There was big money to be made this way. Prisoners of war could also be sold as slaves.

Slave Labor

Men, women, and children were all sold as slaves. Slaves did all kinds of jobs. Some were not too bad, such as being a minor official in government. Others, such as working in the silver mines, were terrible. Conditions in the mines were awful and miners lived very short lives as a result. Even children worked in the mines. Male slaves also had to fight alongside their owners if they went to war.

Wealthy Greek women were assisted by slaves, who carried out all household duties.

Country Hardship

Wealthy Athenians had farms in the country as well as houses in the city. Slaves had to do all the hard labor on farms. They prepared the soil, then planted and later harvested the crops. They made olive oil, wine, and cheese, and cared for animals. It was a tough life and slaves worked outdoors in all kinds of weather.

THE HORRIBLE TRUTH

There were many slaves in ancient Greece.

Of the 350,000 people who lived in Athens, about 100,000 were slaves.

Any Athenian who could afford it had household slaves.

One of the jobs of a farm slave was to harvest crops. This ancient Greek vase shows slaves picking olives.

Domestic Duties

Women in ancient Greece were thought to be less important than men. Even women slaves had a worse time than male slaves. They were not allowed to train in a craft or work outside the home. For most it was a hard life.

A Long, Hard Day

The life of a female household slave was very hard. She was not allowed to leave her master's house, except to go to the market or run errands. Her long day's duties included looking after the children, doing the laundry, shopping for food, preparing meals, and cleaning the house. She also had to care for her mistress. She prepared her clothes, bathed and dressed her, and even styled her hair.

The gravestone of this woman shows her with her female slave. She must have valued her highly.

Spinning and Weaving

A female slave was even expected to spin woolen thread and use it to weave cloth. With this cloth she had to make the family's clothes, and all the other household textiles such as rugs, blankets, and cushions.

This slave is spinning thread to make into clothes for the family.

A Life of Slavery

A female slave was not allowed to marry. Her owner could free her when he died, but if he chose not to, she became the property of his children. And so the slave's hard life went on. If she misbehaved, she would be severely punished. She might be beaten, locked up, or sold to a new owner.

13

Olympic Pankratist

The Olympic Games were first held at Olympia, Greece, in 776 BC. Just like today, Olympic champions were famous and treated as heroes. However, competing in the event called the pankration was a truly horrible job.

Kicking was an important part of pankration. So were arm grips, choking techniques, and throws.

Tough Training

Athletes competed to bring honor to themselves and their families. They had to make the long journey to Olympia on foot, as a pilgrimage. Once the athletes arrived, they had to complete 10 months of hard training while they lived with the other athletes. Special trainers pushed the athletes to the limit, to develop their stamina, strength, endurance, and speed.

This is the *palaestra* at Olympia, where pankration competitors trained and competed. Rooms surrounded a central courtyard covered with sand.

No Fighting Allowed!

The Olympic Games were held every 4 years. During the games a truce was declared between any warring city-states. It was forbidden to attack a pilgrim who was on his way to compete in or watch the games.

Deadly Pankration

Greek boys learned wrestling at school, but the pankration event took that sport to another, gruesome level. It combined wrestling and boxing—and there were hardly any rules. Kicking, punching, and strangling were all allowed. Only biting and gouging the eyes were forbidden! The aim was to throw your opponent to the ground three times. Pankratists were very skilled at grappling, choking, and pinning their opponents on the ground. Competitions sometimes ended only with the death of one competitor and a victory for the other one!

15

Chapter Two
Hard Labor

The ancient Greeks were great builders. They built up their cities as great centers of civilization, with massive temples to their gods and buildings for their government. Yet, who built these great monuments? Many thousands of poor, hardworking laborers!

Building the Parthenon temple took 15 years of hard labor.

Carving Stone

The Acropolis in Athens was the site of the city's main temples. By far the biggest was the temple to the goddess Athena, called the Parthenon. It was built to house a massive statue of the goddess.

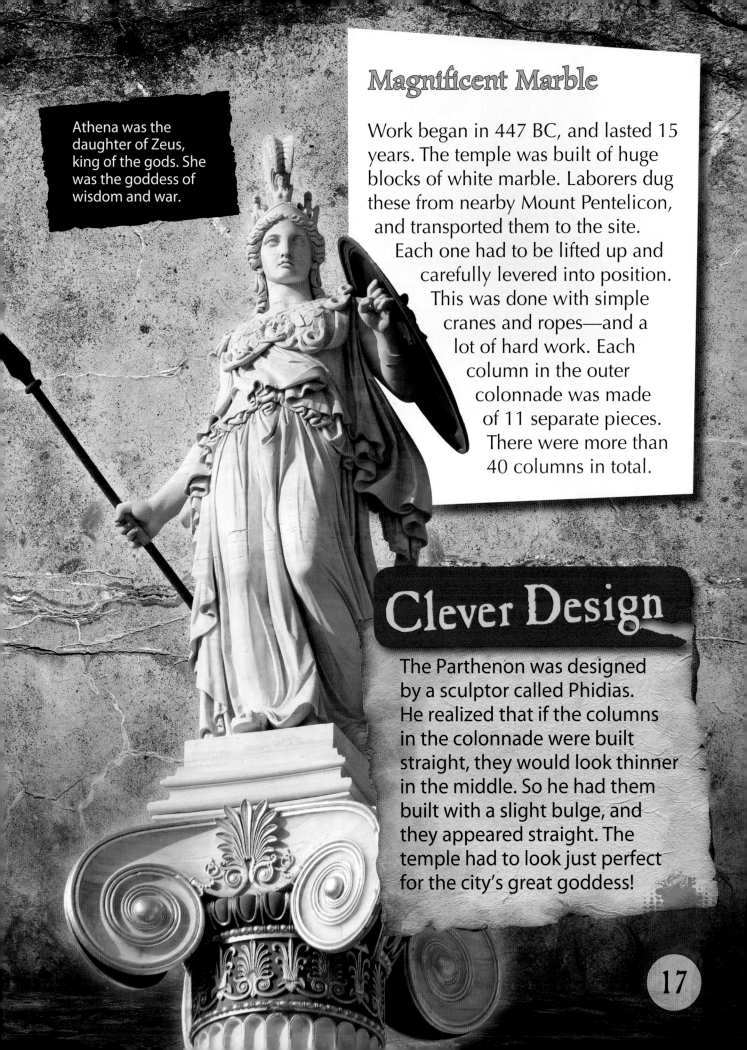

Athena was the daughter of Zeus, king of the gods. She was the goddess of wisdom and war.

Magnificent Marble

Work began in 447 BC, and lasted 15 years. The temple was built of huge blocks of white marble. Laborers dug these from nearby Mount Pentelicon, and transported them to the site. Each one had to be lifted up and carefully levered into position. This was done with simple cranes and ropes—and a lot of hard work. Each column in the outer colonnade was made of 11 separate pieces. There were more than 40 columns in total.

Clever Design

The Parthenon was designed by a sculptor called Phidias. He realized that if the columns in the colonnade were built straight, they would look thinner in the middle. So he had them built with a slight bulge, and they appeared straight. The temple had to look just perfect for the city's great goddess!

Mighty Ship Builder

The Greeks had a strong fleet of ships for controlling the trade routes of the Aegean Sea. They also used ships to travel by sea from one part of the country to another, because inland routes were often over dangerous mountains. The Greeks' most impressive ships were the warships, called *triremes*. These protected the trading ships and fought Greece's enemies. Building these huge vessels was backbreaking work.

It took many men to build the massive Greek triremes.

THE HORRIBLE TRUTH

Triremes were built of wood, about 115 feet (35 m) long, with one tall mast and possibly a second shorter one. With the combined power of two sails and 170 oars, the boats could reach great speeds. Crews were made up of the best oarsmen, whether they were rich or poor. They were not slaves, but free men.

Greek triremes won a great battle against the Persians in the famous Battle of Salamis in 480 BC.

Massive Warships

Triremes were powered by sails and three long rows of oars on either side of the ship. At the front was a massive battering ram. The building of triremes was usually paid for by wealthy citizens. They competed with each other to build the most impressive ship and to attract the best oarsmen. Building each trireme required hundreds of laborers and lots of money. The poor builders also had to make sheds at the harbors, to house the ships during winter when seas were rough.

Hoplite Soldier

All Athenian males served some time in the army when their city was at war. The city-states often fought each other. As a hoplite soldier it was your job to fight to the death, or until the battle was won.

Hoplite soldiers had to pay for their own weapons and armor.

In Formation

Hoplite soldiers were unusual because they were trained to fight in a special formation called a phalanx. This was a very long line, around four to eight soldiers deep. The hoplites stood shoulder to shoulder. When the hoplites marched forward together, no enemy spears or arrows could penetrate their wall of shields.

Attack

When attacking, the first two rows of hoplites thrust their spears at the enemy. The hoplites in the rows behind moved forward, and filled any gaps in the rows as the soldiers fell down dead or injured.

No Room for the Poor

The hoplite soldiers had to have the correct armor and weapons to fight. Without a wall of shields, the hoplite formation of fighting did not work. Armor at the time was very expensive and consisted of a helmet, a round shield, a long spear, and a sword. Poor men couldn't afford this great expense and so were never able to fight with the hoplite soldiers.

Hoplite soldiers had round shields to protect them in battle.

The Spartans

In Sparta, hoplites trained for war from the young age of 7. Boys had to leave their families and live on army barracks, where intensive training began. Spartan hoplites also wore a red cloak over their armor when they went to war.

Chapter Three Ancient Rome

Just like the ancient Greeks, the Roman Empire was one of the greatest civilizations the world has ever known. In the early second century AD, it included most of Europe, North Africa, and part of the Middle East. The city of Rome was the capital of the empire. There, life was comfortable and easy if you were rich. However, for the poor, and for slaves, there were plenty of really horrible jobs to be done.

So Many Jobs

Inscriptions found by archaeologists have recorded 268 different jobs for people in Rome, and 85 in a smaller town, Pompeii. Slaves worked at several different kinds of jobs: in the household, as minor officials in government, as craftsmen, as farm laborers, and as miners. Just as in Greece, the last of these was definitely the worst.

Great building projects, such as this aqueduct in Vatican City, Rome, required hard labor from many hundreds of men.

No Pay for Slaves

Most slaves were not paid for their work. Some earned a little money from selling their craft goods. People who were paid received coins. These were made of silver or gold, and showed the head of the emperor on one side. The same coins were used throughout the empire, which made trading simpler.

Some people, such as soldiers, were paid with money.

Top Job

In AD 1 the city of Rome had a population of more than 1 million. The most powerful job was that of emperor who ruled over millions of people and lived in grand palaces. However, even that could be horrible. Many emperors were poisoned, stabbed, or murdered in other horrible ways by their enemies.

Baths Slave

Going to the public baths was an important part of Roman life. People went not just to get clean but to exercise, do business, socialize, and relax. For the slaves who worked there, however, life was far from fun. It was sweaty, smelly work!

Sweaty Work

The Romans didn't wash with soap. They had a much more horrible way to get clean. First, they would exercise in a gymnasium, or sit around in a steam room, to get really sweaty. Then the job of the slave began. He had to rub oil all over their smelly bodies. Next, he picked up a curved metal scraping tool called a strigil. He used this to scrape all the oil and dirt off the bather's body—gross!

The Romans would wash at public baths like this one in Bath, England.

The slave used this strigil to scrape the dirty oil off the bathers.

Feeding the Furnace

There was another horrible job at the baths. Down below ground, slaves worked constantly to feed the furnaces with wood. This kept the fires burning, to heat the water in the hot baths. It must have been swelteringly hot for the slaves who worked there.

Daily Dirt

After his body had been scraped of dirt, the bather could then take a plunge in a lovely, big bath of cold water. However, the poor slave had to move on to the next dirty body, and start all over again. Men and women usually used the baths at different times of day. Women went in the morning, and men in the afternoon. The slaves, of course, were there all day.

Romans visited a series of bathing rooms in order, from hot and steamy to cool and refreshing.

Telling Fortunes

The Romans had many superstitious beliefs. Before they made an important decision or a journey, they would try to find out whether the gods were in favor of their plans. One way to do this was to consult a fortune-teller.

The Roman Emperor Claudius opened a college for fortune-tellers.

Blood and Guts

A Roman fortune-teller was called a *haruspex*. In some ways, it wasn't too bad a job. There was always plenty of work and people would listen to what you had to say. The downside of the job was that fortune-tellers used horrible techniques to tell the future. To find out the will of the gods, the fortune-teller looked closely at the internal organs of animals that had been sacrificed. Especially revealing were the livers of sheep and chickens. So, if you were a fortune-teller, you would have spent your days fishing around inside dead animals to see what clues you could find—truly gross!

Working Alone

The haruspex, also called a soothsayer, was not a priest. He worked alone, and was not thought to be quite as respectable as a priest. However, soothsayers were used by the Senate, the powerful group of politicians who made many of the most important decisions in the empire. They were also consulted by the army.

A haruspex examined the organs of sacrificed animals to work out the will of the gods and tell the future.

Julius Caesar

Julius Caesar was a general who ruled Rome like a tyrant. It was a haruspex who warned him in 44 BC that harm would come to him on March 15, also called the "Ides of March." On that very date, Caesar was murdered at a meeting of the Senate in Rome. The haruspex was right!

Loathsome Laundry

A fuller was a person who did the laundry in Roman times. For a fuller, wash day was not a pleasant experience. A fuller needed a strong stomach to cope with their working day…

Cleaning with Pee

A Roman city had special places where people brought their clothes to be cleaned. The clothes had to be washed, rinsed, and dried. This is where the fullers worked. Believe it or not, urine is great for cleaning clothes! It was the horrible job of the fullers to collect up people's old pee and put it in large containers. The older the pee, the better it worked. They added water, then the clothes. The worst bit came next. The fullers had to stamp on the clothes with bare feet, to remove the dirt.

Keeping Roman clothes clean was certainly a horrible job.

White clothes were hung on this basket structure to dry.

Pompeii Laundry

A Heavy Responsibility

Being a fuller was a respectable profession, but a pretty horrible one. After rinsing, white clothes were treated with stinking sulfur to make them bright white. The fuller was legally responsible for the clothes in his care. There were penalties for returning the wrong clothes, or damaging them.

Eleven laundry workshops have been found in the remains of the Roman city of Pompeii, in southern Italy. The city was buried under volcanic ash after the eruption of the nearby volcano Vesuvius, in AD 79.

Suffering Slave

The Romans had slaves to do many jobs. Of all these jobs, one of the very worst had to be cleaning up the vomit at mealtimes. That was one of the many tasks given to a poor household slave.

These slaves are pouring out wine from large jars.

All You Can Eat

Wealthy Romans loved to hold dinner parties. They could socialize with friends, watch dancing girls and musicians, and sample the food of their highly valued cook. In fact, the Romans liked their food so much that when they were full they would make themselves sick, just so that they could eat some more! In ancient Rome, it was fine to vomit on the dining room floor. After all, a poor, miserable slave would come and clean up and the diners could start eating again!

Diners reclined on couches around the table.

Dinner Details

The main meal of the day, dinner, began in the afternoon and lasted several hours if it was a dinner party. Guests generally ate while lying on three large couches, arranged around a low dining table. They ate most foods with their hands.

Delicious and Disgusting

Roman dinner dishes could be amazing. It was fashionable to make them look and taste exotic, with sauces, spices, and incredible serving arrangements. Dishes included dormouse, ostrich, and flamingo. A popular sauce was made from rotting fish. The food may have been delicious when eaten, but when vomited it was truly disgusting! As well as cleaning up vomit, slaves also had to wash diners' hands between courses, pour the wine, and clean up late at night after the guests had left.

Chapter Four
Entertainment

The Romans loved having fun. On public holidays, large-scale entertainment productions were put on by the government or important and wealthy citizens, to make themselves popular. Enormous crowds gathered to watch their favorite competitors fight it out in the huge open-air theaters called arenas. For the men fighting, however, it could be a very dangerous day's work.

Thousands of animals were killed in the games. Many venatores died, too.

Animal Hunters

A day at a large arena, such as the Colosseum in Rome, began in the morning with the wild animal hunters. They were called *venatores*. Dangerous wild animals were brought from the four corners of the empire. They included elephants, lions, leopards, and bears. They were kept in cages under the floor of the arena, until the entertainment began.

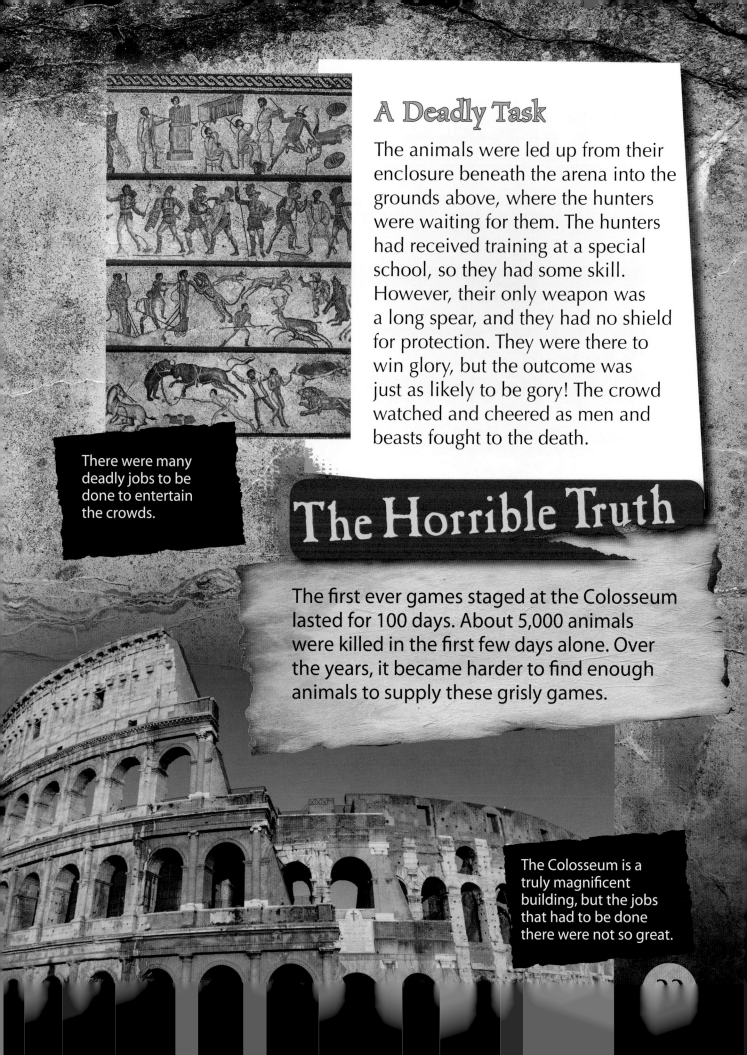

A Deadly Task

The animals were led up from their enclosure beneath the arena into the grounds above, where the hunters were waiting for them. The hunters had received training at a special school, so they had some skill. However, their only weapon was a long spear, and they had no shield for protection. They were there to win glory, but the outcome was just as likely to be gory! The crowd watched and cheered as men and beasts fought to the death.

There were many deadly jobs to be done to entertain the crowds.

The Horrible Truth

The first ever games staged at the Colosseum lasted for 100 days. About 5,000 animals were killed in the first few days alone. Over the years, it became harder to find enough animals to supply these grisly games.

The Colosseum is a truly magnificent building, but the jobs that had to be done there were not so great.

Gory Gladiator

Being a gladiator in ancient Rome was a horrible job. Most gladiators were criminals, prisoners, or slaves. Their training was long and hard, but they were never expected to live for long once they were ready for the arena. Their hard lives would soon come to an end.

A Brutal Show

Gladiators fought in an arena, such as the Colosseum in Rome, in front of up to 50,000 people. They often fought in pairs, in a horribly violent fight to the death. Several fights took place in the arena at once, to make it more of a spectacle for the cheering crowd.

The arena at Nîmes, in the south of France, was an important location for gladiator fights.

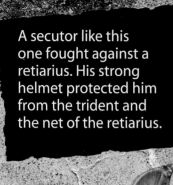

A secutor like this one fought against a retiarius. His strong helmet protected him from the trident and the net of the retiarius.

Different Fighters

There were several different kinds of gladiator. They wore different types of armor and had a range of weapons. A *thracian* had only a helmet, light shield, and curved dagger. The *secutor* and the *hoplomachus* each had a helmet, large sword, and shield. The *retiarius* had only a net and a trident. If he dropped his net, he was almost certain to lose.

Pleasing the Crowd

Gladiator fights were often simply one terrible killing after another. A wounded gladiator would appeal to the huge crowd for mercy. If they liked him they put their thumbs up, and he was spared; down, and he was killed. A lucky few survived and won their freedom. They became popular celebrities, like today's movie stars. For most, though, it was a brutal and terrifying way to die.

Crazy Charioteer

The Romans loved a good show, and a day at the races was one of the most popular of ways to spend free time. Teams of horse-drawn chariots raced around a track at terrifying speed. It was a truly hair-raising and very risky job for the charioteers.

What a Circus!

The venue for chariot racing in Rome was the huge Circus Maximus racetrack. Four teams competed: the Reds, Whites, Greens, and Blues. Spectators supported their favorite team, just like today's sports fans. They even bet on the results. Each team had three chariots, pulled by four horses. They raced seven laps around the track, making terrifyingly tight turns at each end.

These are the remains of the Circus Maximus in Rome.

This is a modern reconstruction of race day at the Circus Maximus in Rome.

Danger and Daring

Charioteers were usually slaves or freed men. They trained hard with their horses to make every second in a race count. They charged out of the starting gates and down the track. Slaves threw water over them to cool them as they tore past. If they took a turn too tightly, the chariot turned over and the charioteers were trampled by the horses of other teams. Many were killed. The winners, however, became very rich and famous and could afford to buy their freedom and enjoy a much better life.

THE HORRIBLE TRUTH

The Circus Maximus was 2,000 feet (600 m) long, with a long central island called the *spina*.

It held 250,000 spectators.

The emperor watched the races from a special box.

Chapter Five
A Long Way from Home

The Roman Empire was huge. Northern Britain, for example, was 1,000 miles from Rome. It was a huge task to keep control of such a large area, which was divided up into smaller areas called provinces. There were horrible jobs to be done everywhere.

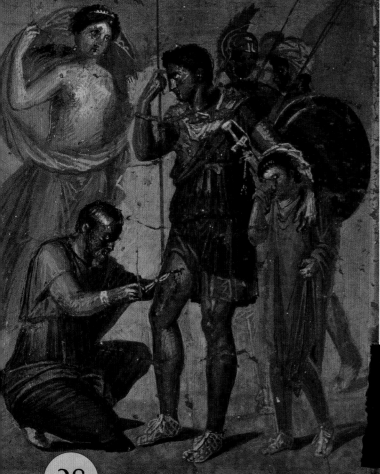

Army Surgeon

The Roman army was extremely successful in battle and its successes allowed the empire to grow. However, fighting soldiers were often wounded. One of the most grisly jobs in the army was as a surgeon. He had only basic tools, and no anesthetic or painkillers. Surgery must have been as unpleasant for the surgeon as it was agonizing for the patient.

During battle, many soldiers were injured and it was the horrible job of the surgeon to treat their wounds.

Instruments and Infection

Removing arrowheads or small objects wasn't too bad. Cutting off badly wounded arms and legs was much, much worse. Metal saws were used to cut through bone, and probably not washed between one operation and the next. A vinegar-soaked sponge helped to stop the flow of blood. If they survived the actual operation, many patients then died from infection in their wounds.

These bronze surgical instruments include scalpels, forceps, saws, and hooks.

Ask the Gods

The Roman god of healing was Aesculapius. There was a temple to Aesculapius on a small island on the River Tiber, in Rome. People went to the temple when they wanted to be cured.

This carving is of Aesculapius and his daughter, Hygieia. It was made in ancient Greece in the fifth century BC.

39

Luckless Legionary

A legionary was a Roman foot soldier. He trained hard and served all over the empire, often in horrible conditions. In the second century AD, there were about 150,000 legionaries in the Roman army.

Terrible Training

Legionaries joined up voluntarily. New recruits had to go through a grueling training for 4 long months, until they were completely exhausted. They had to march at speed, loaded with heavy packs of equipment, armor, and rations. Then there were months of tough weapons training and battle practice. Anyone who failed to reach the required standard was put on a diet of foul-tasting barley and forced to do extra training.

This cold, bleak northern English landscape was a miserable place to be sent in Roman times.

Far Away and Cold

Soldiers were sent to the farthest areas of the empire, to keep the peace and to fight off invaders. The northernmost boundary was at Hadrian's Wall, in northern England. Life was cold and miserable there. Soldiers lived in basic forts that they built themselves as part of the long defensive wall that stretched for miles across the landscape. Barbarians to the north launched frequent attacks. Everyday jobs in these bleak places included breaking up stones to build roads, and cleaning the bathhouse or toilets.

Soldiers trained with heavy wooden swords and shields before they were allowed to use lighter metal ones.

Freezing Facilities

Toilets in Roman times were communal, which meant they were used by many people. Up to a dozen soldiers shared the facilities at this fort on Hadrian's Wall. It was open-air, and often freezing cold. One soldier even wrote home to his mom asking for extra underpants to keep him warm!

41

Miserable Mining

The Romans needed gold. They traded widely, and gold coins were the currency used for that trade. They also liked to make beautiful things out of gold. However, all that precious metal had to be mined from the ground, and that was just about the worst job in ancient Rome—a job for the miserable miners.

Gold jewelry, like these earrings, was prized by wealthy men and women.

Deep and Dark

Deep underground, the miners worked in dark, cramped, and dangerous conditions. One of the worst mines was at Dolaucothi in Wales. Bands of quartz ran through the rock, so narrow tunnels were dug to follow the bands. The gold ore was in the quartz. Miners hacked at the quartz rock using only small picks, in tunnels propped up by wood supports. These often collapsed. These miserable miners were slaves who lived in basic huts near the mine.

Fiendish Fire

Deadly fire was used to release the quartz. Fires were started underground to heat the rock. Then water was thrown at the rock, making it shatter. The rock face collapsed, and splinters of sharp rock flew out in the smoky darkness. The chunks of quartz all had to be loaded into baskets and carried by hand up to the surface. It was backbreaking work. At the surface, the gold flecks were extracted from the quartz.

THE HORRIBLE TRUTH

The Romans mined and used a huge amount of gold for their economy.

Spain alone shipped 1,400 tons (1,270 mt) of gold to Rome every year.

This is the site of an old Roman gold mine in Spain.

The End of the Empire

In the third century AD, the Roman Empire began to lose its strength. Groups of invaders from the north and the east began to attack. The army generals were fighting with each other, and the army wasn't strong enough to hold back the invaders. It was the beginning of the end.

The great building projects created by the poor laborers survived the longest. This is the Pantheon, a temple to all the gods built in the heart of Rome.

Too Big to Survive

The size of the empire had become a problem. It took a huge number of people to try to control the empire, and many people within this system were corrupt. The barbarians from the area of Germany to the north invaded parts of the empire, such as France, and began to settle there. In AD 395, the empire was divided into a Western and Eastern Empire. In AD 476, the last emperor of the Western Empire was overthrown by a barbarian. The age of the Romans was over.

An End to Horrible Jobs?

What changed when the Roman Empire came to a close? In some ways everyday life for many people, such as peasants, probably did not change very much. However, for some people who did horrible jobs, the empire's end meant a big change in their lives. The army was broken up so the soldiers' lives changed drastically. Slavery disappeared and many big landowners lost their estates. The awful entertainments in the Colosseum also came to an end, which was just as well for those poor gladiators!

An End to Peace

Perhaps the biggest change was the end of peace in western Europe. The united, peaceful empire was replaced by many smaller states, which fought each other. Wars meant there was less trade across the region, and so less money was made.

The Eastern Empire continued for another 1,000 years. This was the cathedral of its capital, Constantinople (Istanbul today).

Glossary

archaeologists people who study the past by digging for and examining remains from earlier times

barbarians an uncivilized group of people

boundary something that shows a limit or end

citizens residents of a city or town

city-states areas of Greece during ancient times, the biggest city-state was Athens

civilization the culture of a particular society that has reached an advanced level

colonnade an evenly spaced row of columns

corrupt not honest, or to change from good to bad

culture people's way of life

currency money

emperor ruler of the Roman empire

exotic striking and beautiful

fertile producing crops or vegetation plentifully

forts strong, fortified structures

fuller a person who did laundry

gladiator a man who was trained to fight in armed combat in the arena

haruspex a Roman fortune-teller, also called a soothsayer

invaders a group of people who enter a country to conquer it

legionary a soldier in the Roman army

minor official a person who has minor power

pankration an event at the Olympic Games that combined wrestling and boxing

philosophy the study of the basic ideas about knowledge, truth, right and wrong, nature, religion, and the meaning of life

pilgrim a person who travels to a shrine or holy place to worship

pilgrimage the journey of a pilgrim

quartz a type of rock that was mined for the small pieces of gold it contained

rations a food allowance

Senate a powerful group of politicians during the Roman empire

soothsayer a Roman fortune-teller, also called a haruspex

strigil a metal tool used to remove oil and dirt at the baths

sulfur a chemical used in Roman times to clean clothes

superstitious beliefs or practices resulting in ignorance

trade the buying and selling of goods

trident a spear with three prongs at the end

triremes Greek warships

truce a short rest from fighting

tyrant a ruler who exercises total power cruelly

voluntarily of one's own free will

For More Information

Books

Barber, Nicola. *Ancient Roman Jobs*. New York, NY:
PowerKids Press, 2010.

James, Simon. *Eyewitness Ancient Rome*. New York, NY:
DK Publishing, 2008.

Napoli, Donna Jo. *Treasury of Greek Mythology: Classic
Stories of Gods, Goddesses, Heroes & Monsters*. Washington,
DC: National Geographic Society, 2011.

Pearson, Anne. *Ancient Greece*. New York, NY:
DK Publishing, 2007.

Websites

Find out more about Ancient Greece at:
www.ducksters.com/history/ancient_greece.php

Find out more about Ancient Rome at:
www.ducksters.com/history/ancient_rome.php

Check out these websites about the ancient world:
www.kidspast.com/world-history/0058-ancient-greeks.php
and
www.kidspast.com/world-history/0076-ancient-rome.php

Index